Step by Step

loreen leedy

HOLIDAY HOUSE ✦ NEW YORK

To Linda Bernfeld for her encouraging words

Copyright © 2018 by Loreen Leedy
All Rights Reserved
HOLIDAY HOUSE is registered in the U.S. Patent and Trademark Office.
Printed and Bound in December 2017 at Tien Wah Press, Johor Bahru, Johor, Malaysia.
The artwork was drawn and painted using a computer and digital tablet.
www.holidayhouse.com
First Edition
1 3 5 7 9 10 8 6 4 2
Library of Congress Cataloging-in-Publication Data
Names: Leedy, Loreen, author, illustrator.
Title: Step by step / written and illustrated by Loreen Leedy.
Description: First edition. | New York : Holiday House Publishing, Inc.,
[2018] | Audience: Ages 3-6. | Audience: Pre-school, excluding K.
Identifiers: LCCN 2017019225 | ISBN 9780823439393 (hardcover)
Subjects: LCSH: Animal tracks—Juvenile literature. |
Animals—Infancy—Juvenile literature. | Animals—Locomotion—Juvenile
literature. | LCGFT: Picture books.
Classification: LCC QL768 .L36 2018 | DDC 591.47/9—dc23 LC record available at https://lccn.loc.gov/20170192

Who walks in the mud?

A puppy.

Who waddles
to the pond?

A duckling.

Who stands up
soon after birth?

A fawn.

Who crawls
to the ocean?

A sea turtle
hatchling.

Who hops from here

. . . to there?

A rabbit kitten.

Who walks in
the snow?

A penguin chick.

Who digs holes
in the ground?

An armadillo pup.

Who wears a
borrowed shell?

A hermit crab.

Who warms
up in the sun?

An alligator
hatchling.

Who needs green
leaves to eat?

A woolly
bear caterpillar.

Who hatches from the biggest egg?

An ostrich chick.

Who likes to
play in water?

An elephant calf.

Who learns to
walk on two feet?

A baby!

Newborn puppies are helpless at birth but can soon crawl. After a few weeks they can walk and even run. The toenails often show in a dog's paw prints.

A young whitetail deer is called a **fawn**. It has spots. Shortly after being born it stands up to nurse. Soon it can follow its mother. A deer's foot has two toes and is called a cloven hoof. A deer often walks so that its hind footsteps are inside the track of the front foot.

Sea turtle eggs are hidden in a nest dug on the beach. After hatching, the tiny turtles use their four flippers to crawl as fast as they can to the ocean. Then they swim out to sea.

Hatched on land, **mallard ducklings** can walk within a day. They follow their mother to a nearby body of water such as a pond to find food. The webbing on duck feet can be seen in their tracks.

back

front

Cottontail rabbits are hairless at birth. They grow quickly and live on their own by four or five weeks of age. When hopping, they land on their front feet first, then swing their back feet forward.

* Tracks are not to scale.

Emperor penguins nest in the frigid cold of Antarctica. The father keeps the egg warm on top of his feet. After hatching, the chick stays on the father's feet for about eight weeks before walking on the icy land.

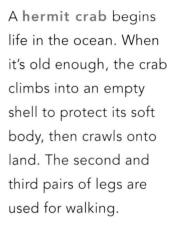

A **hermit crab** begins life in the ocean. When it's old enough, the crab climbs into an empty shell to protect its soft body, then crawls onto land. The second and third pairs of legs are used for walking.

front

Armadillo pups are born in a burrow and stay underground for about three weeks. Once outside, they learn to dig for food with their long, sturdy claws. Armadillos often drag their tails behind them as they travel.

front

New **alligator hatchlings** are ten to twelve inches long. Because reptiles are cold-blooded, they lie in the sun to get warm. Alligators have five toes on each front foot and four toes on each back foot.

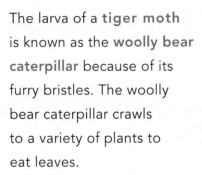

The larva of a **tiger moth** is known as the **woolly bear caterpillar** because of its furry bristles. The woolly bear caterpillar crawls to a variety of plants to eat leaves.

A **newborn elephant calf** weighs over 200 pounds. It can stand and walk shortly after birth, but is wobbly for a few days. Elephants have large toenails on their round feet.

An **ostrich egg** weighs about three pounds and is the largest bird egg. An ostrich chick has two toes on each foot and can walk and feed itself soon after hatching. As an adult, it can run forty miles an hour or more.

Human babies are helpless at birth. Within a few months they start to roll over, sit up, and crawl. At about one year of age, babies can stand up by holding on to a support. With practice, they learn to walk.